Healthy Instant Pot Recipes Made Simple

Super Easy Instant Pot Recipes to Cook Every Day at Home for Keep Body Healthy and Fit

Victoria Carter

Table of Contents

broadly considered a truthful and accurate account of facts and as such, any inattention, use, or misuse of the information in question by the reader will render any resulting actions solely under their purview. There are no scenarios in which the publisher or the original author of this work can be in any fashion deemed liable for any hardship or damages that may befall them after undertaking information described herein. Additionally, the information in the following pages is intended only for informational purposes and should thus be thought of as universal. As befitting its nature, it is presented without assurance regarding its prolonged validity or interim quality. Trademarks that are mentioned are done without written consent and can in no way be considered an endorsement from the trademark holder.

Introduction

Instant pot is a pressure cooker, also stir-fry, stew, and cook rice, cook vegetables and chicken. It's an all-in-one device, so you can season chicken and cook it in the same pan, for example. In most cases, instant pot meals can be served in less than an hour.

Cooking less time is due to the pressure cooking function that captures the steam generated by the liquid cooking environment (including liquids released from meat and vegetables), boosts the pressure and pushes the steam back.

But don't confuse with traditional pressure cookers. The instant pot, unlike the pressure cooker used by grandparents, eliminates the risk of safety with a lid that locks and remains locked until pressure is released.

Even when cooking time is over in the instant pot, you need to take an additional step-to release the pressure.

There are two ways to relieve pressure. Due to the natural pressure release, the lid valve remains in the sealing position and the pressure will naturally dissipate over time. This process takes 20 minutes to over an hour, depending on what is cooked. Low fluidity foods (such as chicken wings) take less time than high fluidity foods such as soups and marinades.

Another option is manual pressure release (also called quick release). Now you need to carefully move the valve to the ventilation position and see that the steam rises slowly and the pressure is released. This Directions is much faster, but foods with high liquid content, such as soups, take about 15 minutes to manually relieve pressure.

Which option should I use? Take into account that even if natural pressure is released, the instant pot is still under pressure. This means that the food will continue to cook while the instant pot is in sealed mode. Manual pressure relief is useful when the dishes are well cooked and need to be stopped as soon as possible.

If the goal is to prepare meals quickly, set the cooking time for dishes that are being cooked in an instant pop and release the pressure manually after the time has passed.

Instant pots (called "Instapot" by many) are one of our favorite cookware because they can handle such a wide range of foods almost easily. Instant pots range from those that work on the basics of pressure cooking to those that can be sterilized using Suicide video or some models can be controlled via Wi-Fi.

In addition, if you want to expand the range of kitchenware, the Instant Pot brand has released an air fryer that can be used to make rotisserie chicken and homemade beef jerky. There is also an independent accumulator device that can be used in instant pots to make fish, steaks and more.

The current icon instant pot works like a pressure cooker and uses heat and steam to quickly cook food. Everything from perfect carnitas to boiled eggs was cooked, but not all ingredients and DIRECTIONSs work. Here are few foods that should not be cooked in classic instant pots.

Instant pots are not pressure fryer and are not designed to handle the high temperatures required to heat cooking oils like crispy fried chicken. Of course, the instant pot is great for dishes like Carnitas, but after removing the meat from the instant pot, to get the final crispness in the meat, transfer it to a frying pan for a few minutes or to an oven top and hot Crispy in the oven.

As with slow cookers, dairy products such as cheese, milk, and sour cream will pack into instant pots using pressure cooking settings or slow cooking settings. Do not add these ingredients after the dish are cooked or create a recipe in Instapot.

There are two exceptions. One is when making yogurt. This is merely possible if you are using an instant pot recipe. The other is only when making cheesecake and following an instant pot recipe.

Although you can technically cook pasta in an instant pot, gummy may appear and cooking may be uneven. To be honest, unless you have a choice, cooking pasta in a stove pot is just as fast and easy and consistently gives you better cooked pasta.

Instead of baking the cake in an instant pot, steam it. The cake is moist-it works for things like bread pudding-but there is no good skin on the cake or on the crunchy edge everyone fights with a baked brownie. However, let's say your desire is to build a close-up or a simple dessert with your family; you can get a damp sponge in about 30 minutes, except during the DIRECTIONS time.

Canning, a technique for cooking and sealing food in a jar, is often done in a pressure cooker. Therefore, it is recommended to create a batch of jam, pickles or jelly in Instapot. Please do not.

With an instant pot, you can't monitor the temperature of what you can, like a normal pressure cooker. In canning, it is important to cook and seal the dishes correctly. Incorrect cooking and sealing can lead to the growth of bacteria that can cause food poisoning.

If you want to avoid canning in an instant pot, some newer models, such as Duo Plus, have a sterilization setting that can clean kitchen items such as baby bottles, bottles and cookware.

Instant Pot Pressure Cooker Safety Tips

Instant Pot is a very safe pressure cooker consisting of various safety mechanisms. do not worry. It will not explode immediately. Most accidents are caused by user errors and can be easily avoided. To further minimize the possibility of an accident, we have compiled a list of safety tips.

1 Don't leave it alone

It is not recommended to leave home while cooking an instant pot. If you have to leave it alone, make sure it is under pressure and no steam is coming out.

2 Do not use KFC in instant pot

Do not fry in an instant pot or other pressure cooker.

KFC uses a commercial pressure fryer specially made to fry chicken (the latest one that operates at 5 PSI). Instant pots (10.5-11.6 PSI) are specially made to make our lives easier.

3 water intake!

Instant pots require a minimum of 1 1/2 cup liquid (Instant Pot Official Number) 1 cup liquid to reach and maintain pressure.

The liquid can be a combination of gravy, vinegar, water, chicken etc.

4 half full or half empty

The max line printed on the inner pot of the instant pot is not for pressure cooking.

For pressure cooking: up to 2/3 full

Food for pressure cooking that expands during cooking (grains, beans, dried vegetables, etc.): up to 1/2

5 Not a facial steamer

Deep cleaning is not performed even if the pressure cooker steam is used once.

When opening, always tilt the lid away from you. Wear waterproof and heat-resistant silicone gloves especially when performing quick release.

6 never use power

 In situations of zero, you should try to force open the lid of the instant pot pressure cooker, unless you want to prevent a light saber from hitting your face.

7 Wash Up & Checkout

If you want to be secured, wash the lid after each use and clean the anti-block shield and inner pot. Make sure that the gasket (silicon seal ring) is in good shape and that there is no food residue in the anti-block shield before use.

Usually silicone seal rings should be replaced every 18-24 months. It is always advisable to keep extra things.

Do not purchase a sealing ring from a third party because it is an integral part of the safety features of the instant ring.

Using sealing rings that have not been tested with instant pot products can create serious safety concerns."

Before use, make sure that the sealing ring is securely fixed to the sealing ring rack and the anti-block shield is properly attached to the vapor discharge pipe.

A properly fitted sealing ring can be moved clockwise or counterclockwise in the sealing ring rack with little force.

With instant pots, the whole family can cook meals in less than 30 minutes. Cooked dishes such as rice, chicken, beef stew, sauce, yakitori can be cooked for 30-60 minutes from the beginning to the end. And yes, you can bake bread in an instant pot.

Old and ketogenic diet fans love instant pots for their ability to `` roast " meat in such a short time, but vegetarians and vegans that can quickly cook dishes such as pumpkin soup, baked potatoes and marinated potato chilis, also highly appreciated oatmeal cream and macaroni and cheese.

Even dried beans, which usually require overnight cooking, can be prepared in 30 minutes to make spicy hummus.

Easy Salmon

Preparation time: 5 minutes.

Cooking time: 20 minutes.

Servings: 2

Ingredients:

2 thick salmon fillets

½ lemon juice

1 clove garlic

Salt and pepper to taste

Olive oil for brushing

Directions:

Preheat the air fryer. Set the time of 5 minutes and the temperature to 2000C.

Wash the salmon slices with lemon juice and season with garlic, salt, and pepper to taste.

Place the salmon with the skin facing down in the basket of the air fryer.

Brush with olive oil. Set the time of 15 minutes and press the power button. Turn salmon slices in half the time to leave cooked equally.

Nutrition:

Energy: 191
Fat: 12.10g
Carbohydrates: 0g
Protein: 20.62g
Sugar: 0g
Cholesterol: 48.10mg

Hake with Roasted Peppers

Preparation time: 5 minutes.

 Cooking time: 15 minutes.

 Servings: 2

Ingredients:

4 large hake fillets

Egg and breadcrumbs

Salt

Ground pepper

Extra virgin olive oil

Roasted and seasoned peppers

Directions:

Roast the peppers in advance and once they are cold, peel and cut.

Chop onion and season with salt, extra virgin olive oil and vinegar.

Season the hake fillets.

Go through beaten egg and then breadcrumbs.

Paint well with extra virgin olive oil.

Place in the basket of the air fryer and select 15 minutes 1800C.

Serve the hake with the roasted peppers.

Nutrition:

Calories: 132

Fat: 4.38g

Carbohydrates: 0.41g

Protein: 21.38g

Sugar: 0.09g

Cholesterol: I78mg

Mushrooms Stuffed with Tuna

Preparation time: 5 minutes.

 Cooking time: 10 minutes.

 Servings: 4

Ingredients:

8 large mushrooms

1 can of tuna

Mayonnaise

Directions:

Remove the trunks to the mushrooms and reserve for another recipe.

Peel the mushrooms and place in the basket of the air fryer, face down.

Select 1600C, 10 minutes.

Take out and let cool.

In a bowl, mix the well-drained tuna with a little mayonnaise, just to make the tuna juicy and compact.

Fill the mushrooms with the tuna and mayonnaise mixture.

Nutrition:

Calories: 150

Fat: 6g

Carbohydrates: 1g

Protein: 8g

Sugar: 0g

Cholesterol: l5mg

Hake Fillets with Salad

Preparation time: 5 minutes.

Cooking time: 20 minutes.

Servings: 4

Ingredients:

8 hake fillets

Flour, egg, and breadcrumbs for breading

1 lettuce

1 bag of canons

Slices of cooked ham

Extra virgin olive oil

Sherry vinegar

Salt

Directions:

Season the hake fillets.

Breaded, passed through flour, beaten egg and breadcrumbs.

Place in the air fryer and paint with oil.

Select 1800C, 20 minutes.

Make hake fillets in batches.

Prepare the salad, in a bowl put the lettuce chopped with the canons and add salt, vinegar and oil.

Bind and add the chopped cooked ham.

Serve the hake fillets with the salad.

Nutrition:

Calories: 132

Fat: 4.38g

Carbohydrates: 0.41g

Protein: 21.38g

Sugar: 0.09g

Cholesterol: 178mg

Hake Breaded with Red Peppers Cream

Preparation time: 5 minutes.

Cooking time: 20 minutes.

Servings: 4

Ingredients:

4 frozen breaded hake fillets

1 large onion

1 large or 2 medium red pepper

200 ml of cooking cream

Extra virgin olive oil

Salt

Ground pepper

Directions:

Cut the onion and pepper in julienne and put it in a pan with a little extra virgin olive oil over medium-low heat to sauté.

Place the hake fillets in the basket of the air fryer and paint with a silicone brush and oil.

Select 1800C about 20 minutes or so.

While the hake fillets are made, return to the peppers. When they are tender, add the cream, salt, and pepper.

Boil so that the cream reduces.

Nutrition:

Calories: 132

Fat: 4.38g

Carbohydrates: 0.41g

Protein: 21.38g

Sugar: 0.09g

Cholesterol: 178mg

Breaded Hake with Green Chili Pepper and Mayonnaise

Preparation time: 5 minutes.

 Cooking time: 20 minutes.

 Servings: 4

Ingredients:

4 breaded hake fillets

Mayonnaise

Green mojito

Extra virgin olive oil

Directions:

Paint the breaded hake fillets with extra virgin olive oil.

Put them in the air fryer basket and select 1800C, 30 minutes.

Meanwhile, put in a bowl 8 teaspoons of mayonnaise and 2 of green mojito. Both the mayonnaise and the green mojito can be homemade or commercial.

Let flirt well.

Serve the breaded hake fillets with the green mojito mayonnaise.

Nutrition:

Calories: 132

Fat: 4.38g

Carbohydrates: 0.41g

Protein: 21.38g

Sugar: 0.09g

Cholesterol: I78mg

Soups and Stews

Chicken Soup

Preparation Time: 10 minutes

Cooking Time: 17 minutes

Servings: 4

Ingredients:

4 chicken breasts, skinless and boneless

2 tablespoons extra virgin olive oil

1 onion, peeled and chopped

3 garlic cloves, peeled and minced

16 ounces chunky salsa

29 ounces canned diced tomatoes

29 ounces chicken stock

Salt and ground black pepper, to taste

2 tablespoons dried parsley

1 teaspoon garlic powder

1 tablespoon onion powder

1 tablespoon chili powder

15 ounces frozen corn

32 ounces canned black beans, drained

Directions:

Put the instant poton Sauté mode, add the oil, and heat it up. Put in the onion, stir, and cook 5 minutes. Add the garlic, stir, and cook for a minute. Put in the chicken breasts, tomatoes, salsa, pepper, onion powder, stock, salt, garlic powder, parsley, and chili powder, stir, cover, and cook on the Soup setting for 8 minutes. Naturally release the pressure for 10 minutes, uncover the Instant Pot, transfer the chicken breasts to a cutting board, shred with 2 forks, and return to pot. Add the beans and corn, Put the instant poton Manual mode and cook for 2-3 minutes. Divide into soup bowls, and serve.

Nutrition:

Calories – 210

Protein – 26 g.

Fat – 4.4 g.

Carbs – 18 g.

Potato and Cheese Soup

Preparation Time: 10 minutes

Cooking Time: 10 minutes

Servings: 6

Ingredients:

6 cups potatoes, cubed

2 tablespoons butter

½ cup yellow onion, chopped

28 ounces chicken stock

Salt and ground black pepper, to taste

2 tablespoons dried parsley

1/8 teaspoon red pepper flakes

2 tablespoons cornstarch

2 tablespoons water

3 ounces cream cheese, cubed

2 cups half and half

1 cup cheddar cheese, shredded

1 cup corn

6 bacon slices, cooked and crumbled

Directions:

Put the instant poton Sauté mode, add the butter and melt it. Put in the onion, stir, and cook 5 minutes. Add half of the stock, salt, pepper, pepper flakes, and parsley and stir. Put the potatoes in the steamer basket, cover the Instant Pot and cook on the Steam setting for 4 minutes. Naturally release the pressure, uncover the Instant Pot, and transfer the potatoes to a bowl. In another bowl, mix the cornstarch with water and stir well. Put the instant potto Manual mode, add the cornstarch slurry, cream cheese, and shredded cheese and stir well. Add the rest of the stock, corn, bacon, potatoes, half and half. Stir, bring to a simmer, ladle into bowls, and serve.

Nutrition:

Calories – 188

Protein – 9 g.

Fat – 7.14 g.

Carbs – 22 g.

Split Pea Soup

Preparation Time: 10 minutes

Cooking Time: 20 minutes

Servings: 6

Ingredients:

2 tablespoons butter

1 pound chicken sausage, ground

1 yellow onion, peeled and chopped

½ cup carrots, peeled and chopped

½ cup celery, chopped

2 garlic cloves, peeled and minced

29 ounces chicken stock

Salt and ground black pepper, to taste

2 cups water

16 ounces split peas, rinsed

½ cup half and half

¼ teaspoon red pepper flakes

Directions:

Put the instant poton Sauté mode, add the sausage, brown it on all sides and transfer to a plate. Put the butter in the Instant Pot and melt it. Add the celery, onions, and carrots, stir, and cook 4 minutes. Mix in the garlic, stir and cook for 1 minute. Add the water, stock, peas and pepper flakes, stir, cover and cook on the Soup setting for 10 minutes. Release the pressure, puree the mix using an immersion blender and Put the instant poton Manual mode. Add the sausage, salt, pepper, and half and half, stir, bring to a simmer, and ladle into soup bowls.

Nutrition:

Calories – 30

Protein – 20 g.

Fat – 11 g.

Carbs – 14 g.

Corn Soup

Preparation Time: 10 minutes

Cooking Time: 15 minutes

Servings: 4

Ingredients:

2 leeks, chopped

2 tablespoons butter

2 garlic cloves, peeled and minced

6 ears of corn, cobs reserved, kernels cut off,

2 bay leaves

4 tarragon sprigs, chopped

1-quart chicken stock

Salt and ground black pepper, to taste

Extra virgin olive oil

1 tablespoon fresh chives, chopped

Directions:

Put the instant poton Sauté mode, add the butter and melt it. Add the leeks and garlic, stir, and cook for 4 minutes. Add the corn, corn cobs, bay leaves, tarragon, and stock to cover everything, cover the Instant Pot and cook on the Soup setting for 15 minutes. Release the pressure, uncover the Instant Pot, discard the bay leaves and corn cobs, and transfer everything to a blender. Pulse well to obtain a smooth soup, add the rest of the stock and blend again. Add the salt and pepper, stir well, divide into soup bowls, and serve cold with chives and olive oil on top.

Nutrition:

Calories – 300

Protein – 13 g.

Fat – 8.3 g.

Carbs – 50 g.

Beef and Rice Soup

Preparation Time: 10 minutes

Cooking Time: 15 minutes

Servings: 6

Ingredients:

1 pound ground beef

3 garlic cloves, peeled and minced

1 yellow onion, peeled and chopped

1 tablespoon vegetable oil

1 celery stalk, chopped

28 ounces beef stock

14 ounces canned crushed tomatoes

½ cup white rice

12 ounces spicy tomato juice

15 ounces canned garbanzo beans, rinsed

1 potato, cubed

Salt and ground black pepper, to taste

½ cup frozen peas

2 carrots, peeled and sliced thin

Directions:

Put the instant poton Sauté mode, add the beef, stir, cook until it browns, and transfer to a plate. Add the oil to the Instant Pot and heat it up. Add the celery and onion, stir, and cook for 5 minutes. Put in the garlic, stir and cook for 1 minute. Add the tomato juice, stock, tomatoes, rice, beans, carrots, potatoes, beef, salt, and pepper, stir, cover and cook on the Manual setting for 5 minutes. Release the pressure, uncover the Instant Pot, and set it on Manual mode. Dash more salt and pepper, if desired, and the peas, stir, bring to a simmer, transfer to bowls, and serve hot.

Nutrition:

Calories – 230

Protein – 3 g.

Fat – 7 g.

Carbs – 10 g.

Chicken Noodle Soup

Preparation Time: 10 minutes

Cooking Time: 12 minutes

Servings: 6

Ingredients:

1 yellow onion, peeled and chopped

1 tablespoon butter

1 celery stalk, chopped

4 carrots, peeled and sliced

Salt and ground black pepper, to taste

6 cups chicken stock

2 cups chicken, already cooked and shredded

Egg noodles, already cooked

Directions:

Put the instant poton Sauté mode, add the butter and heat it up. Put in the onion, stir, and cook 2 minutes. Add the celery and carrots, stir, and cook 5 minutes. Add the chicken and stock, stir, cover the Instant Pot and cook on the Soup setting for 5 minutes. Release the pressure, uncover the Instant Pot, add salt and pepper to taste, and stir. Divide the noodles into soup bowls, add the soup over them, and serve.

Nutrition:

Calories – 100

Protein – 7 g.

Fat – 1 g.

Carbs – 4 g.

Zuppa Toscana

Preparation Time: 10 minutes

Cooking Time: 17 minutes

Servings: 8

Ingredients:

1 pound chicken sausage, ground

6 bacon slices, chopped

3 garlic cloves, peeled and minced

1 cup yellow onion, peeled and chopped

1 tablespoon butter

40 ounces chicken stock

Salt and ground black pepper, to taste

Red pepper flakes

3 potatoes, cubed

3 tablespoons cornstarch

12 ounces evaporated milk

1 cup Parmesan, shredded

2 cup spinach, chopped

Directions:

Put the instant poton Sauté mode, add the bacon, stir, cook until it's crispy, and transfer to a plate. Add the sausage to the Instant Pot, stir, cook until it browns on all sides, and also transfer to a plate. Add the butter to the Instant Pot and melt it. Put in the onion, stir, and cook for 5 minutes. Put in the garlic, stir, and cook for a minute. Pour in ⅓ of the stock, salt, pepper, and pepper flakes and stir. Place the potatoes in the steamer basket of the Instant Pot, cover and cook on the Steam setting for 4 minutes. Release the pressure, uncover the Instant Pot, and transfer the potatoes to a bowl. Add the rest of the stock to the Instant Pot with the cornstarch mixed with the evaporated milk, stir, and Put the instant poton Manual mode. Add the cheese, sausage, bacon, potatoes, spinach, more salt and pepper, if needed, stir, divide into bowls, and serve.

Nutrition:

Calories – 170

Protein – 10 g.

Fat – 4 g.

Carbs – 24 g.

Minestrone Soup

Preparation Time: 10 minutes

Cooking Time: 15 minutes

Servings: 8

Ingredients:

1 tablespoon extra virgin olive oil

1 celery stalk, chopped

2 carrots, peeled and chopped

1 onion, peeled and chopped

1 cup corn kernels

1 zucchini, chopped

3 pounds tomatoes, cored, peeled, and chopped

4 garlic cloves, peeled and minced

29 ounces chicken stock

1 cup uncooked pasta

Salt and ground black pepper, to taste

1 teaspoon Italian seasoning

2 cups baby spinach

15 ounces canned kidney beans

1 cup Asiago cheese, grated

2 tablespoons fresh basil, chopped

Directions:

Put the instant poton Sauté mode, add the oil and heat it up. Put in the onion, stir, and cook for 5 minutes. Add the carrots, garlic, celery, corn, and zucchini, stir, and cook 5 minutes. Add the tomatoes, stock, Italian seasoning, pasta, salt, and pepper, stir, cover, and cook on the Soup setting for 4 minutes. Naturally release the pressure, uncover, add the beans, basil, and spinach. Dash more salt and pepper, if desired, divide into bowls, add the cheese on top, and serve.

Nutrition:

Calories –110

Protein – 5 g.

Fat – 2 g.

Carbs – 18 g.

Chicken and Wild Rice Soup

Preparation Time: 10 minutes

Cooking Time: 15 minutes

Servings: 6

Ingredients:

1 cup yellow onion, peeled and chopped

2 tablespoons butter

1 cup celery, chopped

1 cup carrots, chopped

28 ounces chicken stock

2 chicken breasts, skinless, boneless and chopped

6 ounces wild rice

Red pepper flakes

Salt and ground black pepper, to taste

1 tablespoon dried parsley

2 tablespoons cornstarch

2 tablespoons water

1 cup milk

1 cup half and half

4 ounces cream cheese, cubed

Directions:

Put the instant poton Sauté mode, add the butter and melt it. Add the carrot, onion, and celery, stir and cook for 5 minutes. Add the rice, chicken, stock, parsley, salt, and pepper, stir, cover, and cook on the Soup setting for 5 minutes. Release the pressure, uncover, add the cornstarch mixed with water, stir, and Put the instant poton Manual mode. Add the cheese, milk, and half and half, stir, heat up, transfer to bowls, and serve.

Nutrition:

Calories – 200

Protein – 5 g.

Fat – 7 g.

Carbs – 19 g.

Creamy Tomato Soup

Preparation Time: 10 minutes

Cooking Time: 6 minutes

Servings: 8

Ingredients:

1 yellow onion, peeled and chopped

3 tablespoons butter

1 carrot, peeled and chopped

2 celery stalks, chopped

2 garlic cloves, peeled and minced

29 ounces chicken stock

Salt and ground black pepper, to taste

¼ cup fresh basil, chopped

3 pounds tomatoes, peeled, cored, and cut into quarters

1 tablespoon tomato paste

1 cup half and half

½ cup Parmesan cheese, shredded

Directions:

Put the instant poton Sauté mode, add the butter and melt it. Mix in the onion, carrots, and celery, stir, and cook for 3 minutes. Put in the garlic, stir, and cook for 1 minute. Put in the tomatoes, tomato paste, stock, basil, salt, and pepper, stir, cover, and cook on the Soup setting for 5 minutes. Release the pressure, uncover the Instant Pot and puree the soup using and immersion blender. Add the cheese and half and half, stir, Put the instant poton Manual mode and heat everything up. Divide the soup into soup bowls, and serve.

Nutrition:

Calories – 280

Protein – 24 g.

Fat – 8 g.

Carbs – 32 g.

Tomato Soup

Preparation Time: 10 minutes

Cooking Time: 45 minutes

Servings: 6

Ingredients:

For the roasted tomatoes:

14 garlic cloves, peeled and crushed

3 pounds cherry tomatoes, cut into halves

Salt and ground black pepper, to taste

2 tablespoons extra virgin olive oil

½ teaspoon red pepper flakes

For the soup:

1 yellow onion, peeled and chopped

2 tablespoons olive oil

1 red bell pepper, seeded and chopped

3 tablespoons tomato paste

2 celery ribs, chopped

2 cups chicken stock

1 teaspoon garlic powder

1 teaspoon onion powder

½ tablespoon dried basil

½ teaspoon red pepper flakes

Salt and ground black pepper, to taste

1 cup heavy cream

For serving:

Fresh basil leaves, chopped

½ cup Parmesan cheese, grated

Directions:

Take the tomatoes and garlic in a baking tray, drizzle 2 tablespoons oil, season with salt, pepper and a ½ teaspoon of red pepper flakes, toss to coat, introduce in the oven at 425ºF, and roast for 25 minutes. Take the tomatoes out of the oven and set aside. Put the instant poton Sauté mode, add the oil, and heat it up. Add the onion, bell pepper, celery, salt, pepper, garlic powder, onion powder, basil, the remaining red pepper flakes, stir, and cook for 3 minutes. Add the tomato paste, roasted tomatoes, and garlic and stir. Add the stock, cover the Instant Pot, and cook on the Manual setting for 10 minutes. Release the pressure, uncover the Instant Pot and set it on Sauté mode. Add the heavy cream and blend everything using an immersion blender. Divide in bowls, add basil and cheese on top, and serve.

Nutrition:

Calories – 150

Protein – 4 g.

Fat – 1 g.

Carbs – 3 g.

Carrot Soup

Preparation Time: 10 minutes

Cooking Time: 16 minutes

Servings: 4

Ingredients:

1 tablespoon vegetable oil

1 onion, peeled and chopped

1 tablespoon butter

1 garlic clove, peeled and minced

1 pound carrots, peeled and chopped

1 small ginger piece, peeled and grated

Salt and ground black pepper, to taste

¼ teaspoon brown sugar

2 cups chicken stock

1 tablespoon Sriracha

14 ounces canned coconut milk

Cilantro leaves, chopped, for serving

Directions:

Put the instant poton Sauté mode, add the butter and oil, and heat them up. Put in the onion, stir and cook for 3 minutes. Add the ginger and garlic, stir, and cook for 1 minute. Add the sugar, carrots, salt, and pepper, stir, and cook 2 minutes. Add the sriracha, coconut milk, stock, stir, cover, and cook on the Soup setting for 6 minutes. Naturally release the pressure for 10 minutes, uncover the Instant Pot, blend the soup with an immersion blender, add more salt and pepper, if needed, and divide into soup bowls. Add the cilantro on top, and serve.

Nutrition:

Calories – 60

Protein – 2 g.

Fat – 1 g.

Carbs – 12 g.

Cabbage Soup

Preparation Time: 10 minutes

Cooking Time: 10 minutes

Servings: 4

Ingredients:

1 cabbage head, chopped

12 ounces baby carrots

3 celery stalks, chopped

½ onion, peeled and chopped

1 packet vegetable soup mix

2 tablespoons olive oil

12 ounces soy burger

3 teaspoons garlic, peeled and minced

¼ cup cilantro, chopped

4 cups chicken stock

Salt and ground black pepper, to taste

Directions:

In the Instant Pot, mix the cabbage with the celery, carrots, onion, soup mix, soy burger, stock, olive oil, and garlic, stir, cover, and cook on Soup mode for 5 minutes. Release the pressure, uncover the Instant Pot, add the salt, pepper, and cilantro, stir again well, divide into soup bowls, and serve.

Nutrition:

Calories – 100

Protein – 10 g.

Fat – 1 g.

Carbs – 10 g.

Cream of Asparagus

Preparation Time: 10 minutes

Cooking Time: 25 minutes

Servings: 4

Ingredients:

2 pounds green asparagus, trimmed, tips cut off
and cut into medium pieces

3 tablespoons butter

1 yellow onion, peeled and chopped

6 cups chicken stock

¼ teaspoon lemon juice

½ cup crème fraiche

Salt and ground white pepper, to taste

Directions:

Put the instant poton Sauté mode, add the butter and melt it. Add the asparagus, salt, and pepper, stir, and cook for 5 minutes. Add 5 cups of the stock, cover the Instant Pot, and cook on Soup mode for 15 minutes. Release the pressure, uncover the Instant Pot and transfer soup to a blender. Pulse several times and return to the Instant Pot. Put the instant poton Manual mode, add the crème fraiche, the rest of the stock, salt, pepper, and lemon juice, bring to a boil, divide into soup bowls, and serve.

Nutrition:

Calories – 80

Protein – 6.3 g.

Fat – 8 g.

Carbs – 16 g.

Veggie Noodle Soup

Preparation Time: 5 minutes

Cooking Time: 10 minutes

Servings: 4

Ingredients:

Celery – 4 stalks, chopped into bite-sized pieces

Carrots – 4, chopped into bite-sized pieces

Sweet potatoes – 2, peeled and chopped

Sweet onion – 1, chopped

Broccoli florets – 1 cup

Tomato – 1, diced

Garlic – 2 cloves, minced

Bay leaf – 1

Dried oregano – 1 tsp.

Dried thyme – 1 tsp.

Dried basil – 1 tsp.

Salt – 1 to 2 tsp.

Ground black pepper

Dried pasta – 1 cup

Vegetable stock – 4 cups, plus more as needed

Water – 1 to ½ cups, plus more as needed

Chopped fresh parsley, for garnish

Lemon zest for garnish

Crackers, for serving

Directions:

In the Instant Pot, combine the water, stock, pasta, salt, pepper, basil, thyme, oregano, bay leaf, garlic, tomato, broccoli, onion, sweet potatoes, carrots, and celery.

Cover the Instant Pot.

Cook on High for 3 minutes.

Do a natural release and then a quick release.

Remove the lid and stir the soup.

Discard the bay leaf, garnish and serve.

Nutrition:

Calories – 120

Protein – 8 g.

Fat – 10 g.

Carbs – 22 g.

Carrot Ginger Soup

Preparation Time: 5 minutes

Cooking Time: 10 minutes

Servings: 2

Ingredients:

Carrots – 7 chopped

Fresh ginger – 1-inch, peeled and chopped

Sweet onion – ½, chopped

Vegetable stock – 1 ¼ cups

Salt – ½ tsp.

Sweet paprika – ½ tsp.

Ground black pepper

Cashew sour cream for garnish

Fresh herbs for garnish

Directions:

In the Instant Pot, combine the paprika, salt, stock, onion, ginger, and carrots. Season with pepper.

Cover the Instant Pot.

Cook on High for 3 minutes.

Do a natural release and then a quick release.

Open and blend with a hand mixer until smooth.

Garnish and serve.

Nutrition:

Calories – 85

Protein – 6.7 g.

Fat – 8.5 g.

Carbs – 18 g.

Creamy Tomato Basil Soup

Preparation Time: 5 minutes

Cooking Time: 4 minutes

Servings: 4

Ingredients:

Vegan butter – 2 Tbsp.

Small sweet onion – 1, chopped

Garlic – 2 cloves, minced

Carrot – 1, chopped

Celery – 1 stalk, chopped

Vegetable stock – 3 cups

Tomatoes – 3 pounds, quartered

Fresh basil – ¼ cup, plus more for garnishing

Nutritional yeast – ¼ cup

Salt and ground black pepper

Nondairy milk – ½ to 1 cup

Directions:

Press Sauté on the Instant Pot, add butter and melt.

Put in the garlic and onion and stir-fry for 3 to 4 minutes.

Add celery and carrot and cook 2 minutes more. Stir continuously.

Add the stock and deglaze the pot.

Add salt, yeast, basil, and tomatoes. Stir to mix.

Cover the Instant Pot.

Cook on High for 4 minutes.

Do a natural release than a quick release.

Open and blend with a hand mixer until smooth.

Stir in milk. Taste and adjust seasoning.

Garnish and serve.

Nutrition:

Calories – 70

Protein – 5.6 g.

Fat – 7.4g.

Carbs – 13 g.

Cream of Mushroom Soup

Preparation Time: 5 minutes

Cooking Time: 4 minutes

Servings: 4

Ingredients:

Vegan butter – 2 Tbsp.

Small sweet onion – 1, chopped

White button mushrooms – 1 ½ pound, sliced

Garlic – 2 cloves, minced

Dried thyme – 2 tsp.

Sea salt -1 tsp.

Vegetable stock – 1 ¾ cup

Silken tofu – ½ cup

Chopped fresh thyme for garnishing

Directions:

Press Sauté on the Instant Pot. Melt the butter and add the onion. Stir-fry for 2 minutes. Add the salt, dried thyme, garlic, and mushrooms. Stir-fry for 2 minutes more and press Cancel.

Stir in the stock. Cover the Instant Pot.

Cook on High for 5 minutes.

Meanwhile, process the tofu in a food processor until smooth. Set aside.

Do a natural release, then quick release.

Open and blend with a hand mixer until smooth.

Garnish and serve.

Nutrition:

Calories – 80

Protein – 6.2 g.

Fat – 9 g.

Carbs – 17 g.

Chipotle Sweet Potato Chowder

Preparation Time: 3 minutes

Cooking Time: 2 minutes

Servings: 4

Ingredients:

Vegetable stock – 1 ¼ cups

Lite coconut milk – 1 (14-ounce) can

Sweet potatoes – 2, peeled and diced

Canned chipotle peppers – 2 to 4 (in adobo sauce), diced

Red bell pepper – 1, diced

Small onion – 1, diced

Ground cumin – 1 tsp.

Salt – ½ to 1 tsp.

Frozen sweet corn – 1 ½ cups

Adobo sauce from the canned peppers, to taste

Directions:

Whisk the coconut milk and stock in a bowl. Mix well.

Pour into the Instant Pot. Add the salt, cumin, onion, bell pepper, chipotles, and sweet potatoes. Cover the Instant Pot.

Cook on High for 2 minutes.

Do a natural release, then quick release.

Remove the lid and add the adobo sauce and frozen corn.

Warn the corn and serve.

Nutrition:

Calories – 95

Protein – 8.5 g.

Fat – 9.2 g.

Carbs – 23 g.

Coconut Sweet Potato Stew

Preparation Time: 5 minutes

Cooking Time: 4 minutes

Servings: 4

Ingredients:

Avocado oil – 2 Tbsp.

Sweet onion – ½, diced

Sweet potatoes – 2, peeled and cubed

Garlic – 2 cloves, minced

Salt – 1 to 1 ½ tsp.

Ground turmeric – 1 tsp.

Paprika – 1 tsp.

Ground cumin – ½ tsp.

Dried oregano – ½ tsp.

Chili powder – 1 to 2 dashes

Roma tomatoes – 2, chopped

Lite coconut milk – 1 (14-ounce) can, shaken well

Water – 1 ¼ cups, plus more as needed

Chopped kale – 1 to 2 cups

Directions:

Choose Sauté on the Instant pot and add oil.

Add onion and stir-fry for 3 minutes.

Stir in chili powder, oregano, cumin, paprika, turmeric, salt, garlic, and sweet potatoes. Stir-fry for 1 minute.

Add the water, tomatoes, and coconut milk and mix.

Cover the Instant Pot.

Cook on High for 4 minutes.

Do a natural release than a quick release.

Open and stir in the kale. Mix.

Serve.

Nutrition:

Calories – 105

Protein – 9.3 g.

Fat – 10 g.

Carbs – 25 g.

Italian Vegetable Stew

Preparation Time: 5 minutes

Cooking Time: 7 minutes

Servings: 4

Ingredients:

Olive oil – 2 Tbsp.

Leeks – 2, white and very light green parts only, chopped

Sweet onion – 1, chopped

Carrot – 1, chopped

Celery – 1, sliced

White mushrooms – 1 cup, sliced

Small eggplant – 1, chopped

Garlic – 3, cloves, minced

Yukon gold potatoes – 3, chopped

Roma tomatoes – 3, chopped

Vegetable stock – 4 cups

Dried oregano – 1 tsp.

Salt – ½ tsp. plus more as needed

Torn kale leaves – 2 cups

Ground black pepper

Fresh basil for garnishing

Directions:

Choose Sauté on the Instant Pot and add oil.

Add eggplant, mushrooms, celery, carrot, onion, and leeks. Stir-fry for 2 minutes.

Add the garlic.

Cook 30 seconds more.

Add the salt, oregano, stock, tomatoes, and potatoes.

Cover the Instant Pot.

Cook on High for 7 minutes.

Do a natural release and then a quick release.

Open and stir in the kale.

Taste and adjust seasoning.

Serve.

Nutrition:

Calories – 115

Protein – 10 g.

Fat – 12 g.

Carbs – 28 g.

Spinach Mint Stew

Preparation Time: 5 minutes

Cooking Time: 15 minutes

Servings: 4

Ingredients:

2 cups heavy cream

1 tablespoon lemon juice

1 small onion, chopped

2 cups fresh spinach, chopped

2 garlic cloves, minced

1/2 teaspoon black pepper, (finely ground)

1 tablespoon mint leaves, torn

1 teaspoon salt

1 cup celery leaves, chopped

2 tablespoon butter

1 cup celery stalks, chopped

Directions:

Arrange Instant Pot over a dry platform in your kitchen. Open its top lid and switch it on.

Find and press "SAUTE" cooking function; add the butter in it and allow it to heat.

In the pot, add the onions, garlic, and celery stalks; cook (while stirring) until turns translucent and softened for around 2 minutes.

Add celery leaves and spinach; season to taste and stir-cook for 2-3 minutes.

Add in the heavy cream; gently stir to mix well. Close top lid to create a locked chamber; make sure that safety valve is in locking position.

Find and press "MANUAL" cooking function; timer to 5 minutes with default "HIGH" pressure mode. Allow the pressure to build to cook the ingredients.

After cooking time is over, press "CANCEL" setting. Find and press "QPR" cooking function. This setting is for quick release of inside pressure. Slowly open the lid, stir in the mint and lemon juice. Take out the cooked recipe in serving plates or serving bowls and enjoy the keto recipe.

Nutrition:

Calories – 85

Protein – 7.1 g.

Fat – 8 g.

Carbs – 18.6 g.

Creamy Cauliflower and Sage Soup

Preparation Time: 10 minutes

Cooking Time: 10 minutes

Servings: 4

Ingredients:

1 teaspoon butter

1 large onion, chopped

4 cloves garlic, minced

1 teaspoon ground sage

8 cups cauliflower florets

3 cups low-sodium chicken broth

½ teaspoon salt

Pepper to taste

½ cup unsweetened coconut milk

Directions:

Select the Sauté setting and heat the butter. Mix in the onion and cook until clear, about 3-5 minutes. Add the garlic and sage and cook for 1 minute. Add the cauliflower, chicken broth, salt, and pepper, and stir well.

Press Cancel to reset the cooking Directions. Secure the lid and fix the Pressure Release to Sealing. Select the Pressure Cook or Manual setting and set the cooking time to 10 minutes at high pressure.

Once the timer is done, let sit for at least 10 minutes; the pressure will release naturally. Then switch the Pressure Release to Venting to allow any last steam out.

Open the lid and puree the soup using an immersion blender or by transferring it to a stand blender. Stir in the unsweetened coconut milk and add salt and pepper to taste.

Nutrition:

Calories – 171

Protein – 8.8 g.

Fat – 9.2 g.

Carbs – 18.1 g.

Curried Pumpkin Soup

Preparation Time: 10 minutes

Cooking Time: 5 minutes

Servings: 4

Ingredients:

2 tablespoons butter

1 onion, chopped

2 tablespoons curry powder

1/8 teaspoon cayenne pepper (optional)

4 cups vegetable broth

4 cups low-sodium pumpkin puree

1 tablespoon tamari

Salt to taste

Pepper to taste

1½ cups unsweetened coconut milk

1 teaspoon lemon juice

Optional: ¼ cup roasted pumpkin seeds for serving

Directions:

Select the Sauté setting on the Instant Pot and heat the butter. Add the onion and cook until translucent, 3-4 minutes.

Add the curry powder and cayenne (if using), and stir until fragrant 1-2 minutes. Pour in the vegetable broth and the cup of water. Stir in the pumpkin puree and tamari. Season to taste with salt and pepper.

Press Cancel to reset the cooking Directions. Secure the lid and fix the Pressure Release to Sealing. Select the Pressure Cook or Manual setting and set the cooking time to 5 minutes at high pressure.

Once done, set aside for at least 10 minutes; the pressure will release naturally. Then switch the Pressure Release to Venting to allow any last steam out.

Open the lid and puree the soup using an immersion blender or by transferring it to a stand blender. Stir in the unsweetened coconut milk and add salt and pepper to taste.

Ladle into bowls and top with roasted pumpkin seeds, if desired.

Nutrition:

Calories – 340

Protein – 5.8 g.

Fat – 24.9 g. Carbs – 30.9 g.

My Signature Lemon Chicken Soup

Preparation Time: 10 minutes

Cooking Time: 6 minutes

Servings: 4

Ingredients:

1 tablespoon olive oil

1 medium onion, chopped

3 cloves garlic, roughly chopped

2 medium carrots, peeled and sliced

6 stalks celery, sliced

8 cups fat-free chicken broth

1 teaspoon dried thyme

Salt to taste

Pepper to taste

1½ lbs. boneless skinless chicken breasts

4 oz. whole wheat spaghetti, broken in 1-inch pieces

1 bunch kale, stemmed and roughly chopped, to yield 1.5 cups

2 lemons, juiced

Optional: lemon wedges for serving

Directions:

Select the Sauté setting and heat the olive oil. Add the onion, garlic, carrots, and celery and sauté for 4-6 minutes. Add the chicken broth and thyme. Add salt and pepper to taste. Add the chicken breasts and stir well.

Press Cancel to reset the cooking Directions. Secure the lid and fix the Pressure Release to Sealing. Select the Soup setting and set the cooking time to 6 minutes at high pressure.

Once done, set aside for at least 10 minutes; the pressure will release naturally. Then switch the Pressure Release to Venting to allow any last steam out.

Open the lid andtake out the chicken and shred. Add the broken spaghetti and stir; cook for time indicated on package. Add the chicken back to the pot and stir in the kale and lemon juice. Ladle into bowls and serve with an extra squeeze of lemon, drizzle of olive oil, or fresh cracked pepper.

Nutrition:

Calories – 388

Protein – 45 g.

Fat – 7 g., Carbs – 35.1 g.

Fuss-Free French Onion Soup

Preparation Time: 5 minutes

Cooking Time: 20 minutes

Servings: 4

Ingredients:

3 tablespoons unsalted butter

3 large yellow onions, halved and then thinly sliced

2 tablespoons balsamic vinegar

6 cups beef broth

2 large sprigs fresh thyme

1 teaspoon salt

Directions:

Select the Sauté setting and heat the butter. Add the onions and stir constantly until completely cooked down and caramelized. This can take 20-30 minutes or more, depending on your onions and the heat of your Instant Pot. You're looking for a deep caramel color. If the onions begin to blacken at the edges, use the Adjust button to reduce the heat to Less.

Once the onions have caramelized, add the balsamic vinegar, red wine vinegar, broth, thyme, and salt, and scrape up any browned bits from the bottom of the pot.

Press Cancel to reset the cooking Directions. Secure the lid and fix the Pressure Release to Sealing. Select the Soup setting and set the cooking time to 10 minutes at high pressure. Once done, set aside for at least 10 minutes; the pressure will release naturally. Then switch the Pressure Release to Venting to allow any last steam out.

Open the Instant Pot and discard the thyme stems. Flavor with salt and pepper to taste and serve warm.

Nutrition:

Calories – 151

Protein – 5.5 g.

Fat – 9.4 g.

Carbs – 11.5 g.

Creamy Broccoli and Apple Soup

Preparation Time: 5 minutes

Cooking Time: 5 minutes

Servings: 4

Ingredients:

2 tablespoons butter

3 medium leeks, white parts only (frozen is fine!)

2 shallots, chopped, about 3 tablespoons

1 large head broccoli, cut into florets

1 large apple, peeled, cored, and diced

4 cups vegetable broth

1 cup unsweetened coconut milk

Pepper to taste

Salt to taste

Optional: ¼ cup walnuts, toasted

Optional: ¼ cup coconut cream

Directions:

Select the Sauté setting and heat the butter. Add the leeks and shallots and cook, stirring constantly, until softened, 4-6 minutes. Add the broccoli and apple and sauté another 5-6 minutes. Add the vegetable broth and stir well.

Press Cancel to reset the cooking Directions. Secure the lid and fix the Pressure Release to Sealing. Select the Pressure Cook or Manual setting and set the cooking time to 5 minutes at high pressure.

Once done, set aside for at least 10 minutes; the pressure will release naturally. Then switch the Pressure Release to Venting to allow any last steam out.

Open the lid and puree the soup using an immersion blender or by transferring it to a stand blender. Stir in the unsweetened coconut milk and add salt and pepper to taste.

Ladle into bowls and top with toasted walnuts or a drizzle of coconut cream.

Nutrition:

Calories – 259

Protein – 6.8 g.

Fat – 14.3 g.

Carbs – 32.3 g.

Immune-Boost Chard and Sweet Potato Stew

Preparation Time: 10 minutes

Cooking Time: 8 minutes

Servings: 2

Ingredients:

2 tablespoons olive oil

1 tsp cumin seeds, or 1 tsp ground cumin

1 medium onion, diced

2 medium sweet potatoes, peeled and in ½ inch cubes

½ teaspoon turmeric

1 tablespoon fresh ginger, peeled and minced

1 teaspoon salt

1 teaspoon ground coriander

2 cups vegetable broth

1 bunch Swiss chard (about 12 oz)

Optional: lemon wedges for serving

Directions:

Select the Sauté setting and heat the olive oil. Mix inthe onion and cook until clear, 3-5 minutes. If using cumin seeds, add them now and toast them for 1-3 minutes, until fragrant. Otherwise, add the ground cumin in the next step.

Add the sweet potato, ground cumin (if using), ginger, turmeric, coriander, and salt and cook for 3-4 minutes. Add the vegetable broth and chard. Add more salt and pepper if needed.

Press Cancel to reset the cooking Directions. Secure the lid and fix the Pressure Release to Sealing. Select the Pressure Cook or Manual setting and set the cooking time to 8 minutes at high pressure.

Once done, set aside for at least 10 minutes; the pressure will release naturally. Then switch the Pressure Release to Venting to allow any last steam out.

Scoop into bowls and serve warm with a squeeze of lemon juice, if desired.

Nutrition:

Calories – 308

Protein – 6.2 g.

Fat – 14.4 g., Carbs – 42.6 g.

Moroccan Lentil Soup

Preparation Time: 10 minutes

Cooking Time: 10 minutes

Servings: 4

Ingredients:

1 tablespoon olive oil

1 small onion, chopped

3 cloves garlic, minced

3/4 lb. ground turkey

1 tablespoon cumin

1 teaspoon garlic powder

1 teaspoon chili powder

1 teaspoon salt, plus more to taste

¼ teaspoon cinnamon

Pepper to taste

5 cups beef broth

1 cup green or brown lentils

Directions:

Select the Sauté setting and heat the olive oil. Put in the onion and garlic and sauté until fragrant, 2-3 minutes. Add the ground beef and cumin, garlic powder, chili powder, salt, cinnamon, and pepper. Cook until very well-browned and beginning to sear. Add the beef broth and scrape up any browned bits from the bottom of the pot. Add the lentils and stir well.

Press Cancel to reset the cooking Directions. Secure the lid and fix the Pressure Release to Sealing. Select the Soup setting and set the cooking time to 10 minutes at high pressure. Once done, set aside for at least 10 minutes; the pressure will release naturally. Then switch the Pressure Release to Venting to allow any last steam out.

Open the Instant Pot and taste; add more salt and pepper to taste. Ladle into bowls and serve with a drizzle of olive oil or fresh cracked pepper.

Nutrition:

Calories – 364

Protein – 31.3 g.

Fat – 12 g.

Carbs – 32.2 g.

Salmon Meatballs Soup

Preparation Time: 6 minutes

Cooking Time: 10 minutes

Servings: 5

Ingredients:

2 cups hot water

2 beaten large eggs

1 lb. ground salmon

2 minced garlic cloves

2 tbsps. butter

Directions:

In a bowl, mix butter, garlic, eggs and salmon.

Apply a seasoning of pepper and salt.

Combine the mixture and use your hands to form small balls.

Place the fish balls in the freezer to set for 2 hours or until frozen.

Pour the hot water in the Instant Pot and drop in the frozen fish balls.

Apply pepper and salt for seasoning.

Set lid in place and ensure vent is on "Sealing."

On "Manual" mode, set timer to 10 minutes.

Nutrition:

Calories – 199

Protein – 13.3 g.

Fat – 19.4 g.

Carbs – 0.6 g.

Turmeric Chicken Soup

Preparation Time: 6 minutes

Cooking Time: 15 minutes

Servings: 3

Ingredients:

1 bay leaf

½ cup coconut milk

2½ tsps. turmeric powder

4 cups water

3 boneless chicken breasts

Directions:

Place all ingredients in the Instant Pot.

Give a good stir to mix everything.

Set lid in place and ensure vent points to "Sealing."

Set to "Poultry" mode and set timer to 15 minutes.

Do natural pressure release.

Nutrition:

Calories – 599

Protein – 46.8 g.

Fat – 61.4 g.

Carbs – 3.8 g.

Egg Drop Soup with Shredded Chicken

Preparation Time: 6 minutes

Cooking Time: 15 minutes

Servings: 6

Ingredients:

4 beaten eggs

3 cups shredded chicken

2 tbsps. coconut oil

1 chopped celery

1 minced onion

Directions:

Choose the "Sauté" button on the Instant Pot and heat the oil.

Sauté the onion and celery for 2 minutes or until fragrant.

Add the chicken and 4 cups water.

Apply pepper and salt for seasoning.

Set lid in place and ensure vent points to "Sealing."

Press the "Poultry" button and adjust the time to 10 minutes.

Do natural pressure release.

Once the lid is open, press the "Sauté" button and allow the soup to simmer.

Very gently, gradually pour in the beaten eggs and allow to simmer for 3 more minutes.

Nutrition:

Calories – 154

Protein – 9.6 g.

Fat – 12.8 g.

Carbs – 2.9 g.

Asian Egg Drop Soup

Preparation Time: 6 minutes

Cooking Time: 9 minutes

Servings: 3

Ingredients:

2 beaten eggs

1 tsp. grated ginger

3 cups water

2 cups chopped kale

3 tbsps. coconut oil

Directions:

Place all ingredients except for the beaten eggs in the Instant Pot.

Apply pepper and salt for seasoning.

Set lid in place and ensure vent points to "Sealing."

On "Manual" mode, set timer to 6 minutes.

Do natural pressure release.

Once the lid is open, press the "Sauté" button and allow the soup to simmer.

Very gently, gradually pour in the beaten eggs and allow to simmer for 3 more minutes.

Nutrition:

Calories – 209

Protein – 6.5 g.

Fat – 20.3 g.

Carbs – 1.7 g.

Leek and Salmon Soup

Preparation Time: 6 minutes

Cooking Time: 10 minutes

Servings: 4

Ingredients:

1 lb. sliced salmon

1 ¾ cup coconut milk

2 tbsps. avocado oil

3 minced garlic cloves

4 trimmed and chopped leeks

Directions:

Place all ingredients in the Instant Pot.

Apply pepper and salt for seasoning.

Stir to combine all ingredients.

Set lid in place and ensure vent points to "Sealing."

On "Manual" mode, cook for 10 minutes.

Nutrition:

Calories – 535

Protein – 27.3 g.

Fat – 40.9 g.

Carbs – 19.5 g.

Thai Coconut Soup

Preparation Time: 6 minutes

Cooking Time: 6 minutes

Servings: 2

Ingredients:

6 oz. shrimps

1 cup fresh cilantro

2 cups water

3 kaffir limes

1 ½ cups organic coconut milk

Directions:

In the instant pot, add in all ingredients excluding cilantro.

Set lid in place and ensure vent points to "Sealing."

While on "Manual" mode, set timer to 6 minutes.

Do natural pressure release.

Once the lid is open, garnish with the fresh cilantro.

Nutrition:

Calories – 517

Protein – 21.9 g.

Fat – 44.6 g. Carbs – 15.4 g.

Ginger Halibut Soup

Preparation Time: 6 minutes

Cooking Time: 12 minutes

Servings: 4

Ingredients:

2 cups water

2 tbsps. minced fresh ginger

2 tbsps. coconut oil

1 lb. sliced halibut

1 chopped large onion

Directions:

Choose the "Sauté" button on the Instant Pot and heat the oil.

Sauté the onion until fragrant.

Pour in the water and the rest of the ingredients.

Apply pepper and salt for seasoning.

Set lid in place and ensure vent points to "Sealing."

While on "Manual" mode, set timer to 10 minutes.

Nutrition:

Calories – 259

Protein – 10.9 g.

Fat – 22.8 g., Carbs – 7.9 g.

Salmon Head Soup

Preparation Time: 6 minutes

Cooking Time: 12 minutes

Servings: 1

Ingredients:

1 sliced onion

3-inch slivered ginger piece

4 tbsps. coconut oil

1 salmon head

3 cups water

Directions:

Choose the "Sauté" button on the Instant Pot and heat the oil.

Sauté the onion until fragrant.

Pour in the water and add the salmon head and ginger.

Apply pepper and salt for seasoning.

Set lid in place and ensure vent points to "Sealing."

While on "Manual" mode, set timer to 10 minutes.

Do quick pressure release.

Nutrition:

Calories – 474

Protein – 15.3 g.

Fat – 54.4 g.

Carbs – 1.8 g.

Salmon Stew

Preparation Time: 6 minutes

Cooking Time: 13 minutes

Servings: 3

Ingredients:

48 oz. salmon fillets

3 cups spinach leaves

3 tbsps. olive oil

3 cups water

3 minced garlic cloves

Directions:

Choose the "Sauté" button on the Instant Pot and heat the olive oil.

Sauté the garlic until fragrant.

Add the water and salmon fillets. Apply pepper and salt for seasoning.

Set lid in place and ensure vent points to "Sealing."

While on "Manual" mode, set timer to 10 minutes.

Do quick pressure release.

Once the lid is open, press the "Sauté" button and add the spinach.

Allow to simmer for 3 minutes.

Nutrition:

Calories – 825

Protein – 46.1 g.

Fat – 94.5 g.

Carbs – 2.1 g.

Coconut Seafood Soup

Preparation Time: 6 minutes

Cooking Time: 8 minutes

Servings: 5

Ingredients:

1 cup coconut milk

10 peeled and deveined shrimps

1 crushed thumb-size ginger

4 tilapia fillets

2 cups water

Directions:

Place all ingredients in the Instant Pot.

Stir in pepper and salt.

Set lid in place and ensure vent points to "Sealing."

While on "Manual" mode, set timer to 8 minutes.

Nutrition:

Calories – 238

Protein – 13.6 g.

Fat – 28.8 g.

Carbs – 2.7 g.

Poached Egg Soup

Preparation Time: 6 minutes

Cooking Time: 36 minutes

Servings: 2

Ingredients:

Pepper

Salt

1 lb. chicken bones

1 chopped romaine lettuce head

2 whole eggs

Directions:

Place 2 cups water and chicken bones in the Instant Pot.

Set lid in place and ensure vent points to "Sealing."

Set to "Poultry" mode and the timer to 30 minutes.

Do quick pressure release.

Take the bones out and discard.

Press the "Sauté" button and allow the soup to simmer.

Once simmered, carefully crack the eggs open and stir for 3 minutes.

Add the lettuce and season with salt and pepper.

Allow to simmer for 3 more minutes.

Nutrition:

Calories – 443

Protein – 58.3 g.

Fat – 39.2 g.

Carbs – 4.3 g.

Simple Chicken and Kale Soup

Preparation Time: 6 minutes

Cooking Time: 20 minutes

Servings: 4

Ingredients:

1 lb. boneless chicken breasts

4 cups chopped kale

3 tbsps. coconut oil

2 chopped celery stalks

1 diced onion

Directions:

Choose the "Sauté" button on the Instant Pot and heat the oil.

Sauté the onions and celery until fragrant.

Add the chicken breasts and sear for 2 minutes on each side.

Pour in 3 cups water and Apply pepper and salt for seasoning.

Set lid in place and ensure vent points to "Sealing."

Set to "Poultry" mode and the timer to 15 minutes.

Use a natural pressure release and open the lid.

Once the lid is open, press the "Sauté" button and add the kale.

Allow to simmer for 3 minutes.

Nutrition:

Calories – 303

Protein – 20.8 g.

Fat – 29.3 g.

Carbs – 2.2 g.

Leftover Shredded Chicken Soup

Preparation Time: 6 minutes

Cooking Time: 12 minutes

Servings: 3

Ingredients:

7 cups water

2 cups shredded leftover chicken meat

2 tbsps. coconut oil

8 minced garlic cloves

1 chopped onion

Directions:

Choose the "Sauté" button on the Instant Pot and heat the oil.

Sauté the onions and garlic until fragrant.

Add the chicken meat and Apply pepper and salt for seasoning.

Pour in the water. Season with more salt and pepper.

Set lid in place and ensure vent points to "Sealing."

While on "Manual" mode, set timer to 10 minutes.

Nutrition:

Calories – 356

Protein – 23.4 g.

Fat – 32.1 g.

Carbs – 2.5 g.

Cream of Broccoli Soup

Preparation Time: 6 minutes

Cooking Time: 34 minutes

Servings: 5

Ingredients:

1 sliced small avocado

1 tsp. paprika powder

½ lb. chicken bones

2 heads broccoli florets

4 cups water

Directions:

Place the chicken bones and water in the Instant Pot.

Apply pepper and salt for seasoning

Set lid in place and ensure vent points to "Sealing."

While on "Manual" mode, set timer to 30 minutes.

Do quick pressure release.

Once the lid is open, discard the bones.

Stir in the broccoli.

Close the lid once more and choose the "Manual" button and cook for 4 minutes.

Do quick pressure release.

Transfer all contents into a blender then add avocado slices.

Pulse until smooth and set in a bowl.

Apply a sprinkle of paprika powder.

Nutrition:

Calories – 118

Protein – 7.3 g.

Fat – 10.3 g.

Carbs – 1.9 g.

Turkey with Ginger and Turmeric Soup

Preparation Time: 6 minutes

Cooking Time: 17 minutes

Servings: 4

Ingredients:

1 lb. chopped turkey meat

3 tbsps. coconut oil

1 tsp. turmeric powder

1 sliced thumb-size ginger

2 chopped stalks of celery

Directions:

Choose the "Sauté" button on the Instant Pot and heat the oil.

Stir in the celery, ginger, and turmeric powder until fragrant.

Add the turkey meat and stir for another minute.

Pour in 3 cups of water and Apply pepper and salt for seasoning.

Set lid in place and ensure vent points to "Sealing."

While on "Manual" mode, set timer to 15 minutes. Do natural pressure release.

Nutrition:

Calories – 287

Protein – 22.8 g.

Fat – 24.3 g.

Carbs – 0.8 g.

Conclusion

When you are on a diet trying to lose weight or manage a condition, you will be strictly confined to follow an eating plan. Such plans often place numerous demands on individuals: food may need to be boiled, other foods are forbidden, permitting you only to eat small portions and so on.

On the other hand, a lifestyle such as the Mediterranean diet is entirely stress-free. It is easy to follow because there are almost no restrictions. There is no time limit on the Mediterranean diet because it is more of a lifestyle than a diet. You do not need to stop at some point but carry on for the rest of your life. The foods that you eat under the Mediterranean model include unrefined cereals, white meats, and the occasional dairy products.

The Mediterranean lifestyle, unlike other diets, also requires you to engage with family and friends and share meals together. It has been noted that communities around the Mediterranean spend between one and two hours enjoying their meals. This kind of bonding between family members or friends helps bring people closer together, which helps foster closer bonds hence fewer cases of depression, loneliness, or stress, all of which are precursors to chronic diseases.

You will achieve many benefits using the Instant Pot Pressure Cooker. These are just a few instances you will discover in your Mediterranean-style recipes:

Pressure cooking means that you can (on average) cook meals 75% faster than boiling/braising on the stovetop or baking and roasting in a conventional oven.

This is especially helpful for vegan meals that entail the use of dried beans, legumes, and pulses. Instead of pre-soaking these ingredients for hours before use, you can pour them directly into the Instant Pot, add water, and pressure cook these for several minutes. However, always follow your recipe carefully since they have been tested for accuracy.

Nutrients are preserved. You can use your pressure-cooking techniques using the Instant Pot to ensure the heat is evenly and quickly distributed.

It is not essential to immerse the food into the water. You will provide plenty of water in the cooker for efficient steaming. You will also be saving the essential vitamins and minerals. The food won't become oxidized by the exposure of air or heat. Enjoy those fresh green veggies with their natural and vibrant colors.

The cooking elements help keep the foods fully sealed, so the steam and aromas don't linger throughout your entire home. That is a plus, especially for items such as cabbage, which throws out a distinctive smell.

You will find that beans and whole grains will have a softer texture and will have an improved taste. The meal will be cooked consistently since the Instant Pot provides even heat distribution.

You'll also save tons of time and money. You will be using much less water, and the pot is fully insulated, making it more energy-efficient when compared to boiling or steaming your foods on the stovetop. It is also less expensive than using a microwave, not to mention how much more flavorful the food will be when prepared in the Instant Pot cooker.

You can delay the cooking of your food items so you can plan ahead of time. You won't need to stand around as you await your meal. You can reduce the cooking time by reducing the 'hands-on' time. Just leave for work or a day of activities, and you will come home to a special treat.

In a nutshell, the Instant Pot is:

Easy To Use Healthy recipes for the entire family are provided.

You can make authentic one-pot recipes in your Instant Pot.

If you forget to switch on your slow cooker, you can make any meal done in a few minutes in your Instant Pot.

You can securely and smoothly cook meat from frozen.

It's a laid-back way to cook. You don't have to watch a pan on the stove or a pot in the oven.

The pressure cooking procedure develops delicious flavors swiftly.

CPSIA information can be obtained
at www.ICGtesting.com
Printed in the USA
BVHW081956260421
605884BV00013B/397

9 781801 835978